Printed in Great Britain
by Amazon

35148711R00066